# Millionaire Hustle

## The Secrets on How to Promote Yourself

# Koocie Montgomery

# Millionaire Hustle

The Secrets on How to Promote Yourself

*Published in the United States of America*

ISBN: 978-1519478566
$14.95

# Table of Contents

# Dedication

I dedicate this book to my Lord and Savior who has so dearly blessed me beyond all measure. Holy Spirit speak to those who have an open ear. In Jesus name. Amen

# *Introduction*

When doing business, you cannot afford not to have this book. Millionaire Hustle is design to teach you the valuable marketing skills that I picked up on my journey toward success. I am not just writing this book to make a profit, I am writing this book to help you become a millionaire. If you feel as if you cannot become a millionaire, then this book is not for you. However, if you have a burning desire to become more than what you are right now, then this book is for you. This book is design to take you beyond your self-imposed limitations to bring about the true success that's already within you. And, you don't have to go broke trying to make your dream happen—I am going to give you some great information that's not going to cost you an arm & a leg. However, it is going to cost you some "TIME."

The world of marketing has become so expensive and the average person with a great idea cannot afford to market it. Some people are losing money marketing, some people cannot make money without marketing, and some people lose their business because of marketing or the lack thereof. This is an epidemic—we are all going to make mistakes in life, but why does it have to cost us our dream or passion?

God has blessed me with the experience and now I am sharing it with you. Millions of people have dreams, desires and goals; yet, they lack the ability to market it—so they give up, only to build the dream of someone else! Giving up is not an option when you could become the next millionaire by using some of these basic principles of marketing. "Millionaire Hustle" is a $0 marketing strategy program.

I guarantee that this book will help you market your business or idea without spending every dime that you have. Today is your day to break free of the marketing madness—it's time for you to take control of your own destiny. The driving force of our passion resides in our ability to do what others do not have the courage to do. Living your dream or passion takes a risk and so does living your life building someone else's dream. If you feel as if you are worth every dime you spend, this book is a must have. And, whether you are marketing your business or whether you are marketing yourself—THIS BOOK IS FOR YOU!

# Chapter 1
## Marketing with Zero Fluff

Teaching others how to fish for their own substance is the most sustaining way to share the many dimensions of acknowledgement. I have always heard the cliché, "Give credit where credit is due." Who doesn't want to be acknowledged; actually, it feels good to receive credit whether it's just or unjust. However, giving credit where there's no effort, changes this cliché dramatically. Out of all due respect, there is another cliché saying, "Give a man a fish and he will eat for a day; teach a man how to fish and he will eat for a lifetime."

Fishing is strategically taking what we have in or around our life to solve a temporary or long-term problem. It doesn't matter whether or not the problem resides within self or with others, fishing for our own stuff will help eliminate the victim mentality, giving us the upper-hand on acknowledging our short-comings as well as our strengths.

There is greatness in everyone and it's our duty to share what we have to help bring forth something positive in someone else, while taking a step back to allow them to shine. Listen, true leaders give credit where credit is due and they also teach others how to fish for their own substance expecting nothing in return. In my opinion, you can't go wrong in rightfully sharing, respecting and serving others regardless of how they feel about you or vice versa. However, if you never do anything to better yourself, then nothing ever happens.

Now, in order to make things happen, we need to learn how to market where we are right now and polish up our game to better suit where we are going. Marketing is key and if we don't have it, the doors of opportunity can and will be locked on a great product or service. Nothing can be bought or sold if people do not know about us or our product, making it very important to build the awareness of those who desire what we have. Of course, marketing can get pretty expensive, but the goal of this book is to keep our expenses to a minimum while maximizing the value and availability of what we have to offer without going broke doing so. *Millionaire Hustle* is not going to come to us by luck—it's going to come to us by skill. Without marketing, we will not survive for long in the business world. This book is going to teach you how to find your niche and how to work it to your advantage. Now, in order to do so, we must track our channels of marketing strategically by finding out what works for our business and what will not.

Our marketing plan is not the same as our business plan—our marketing plan helps us fine-tune our ability to promote our passion. Here are a few nuggets of information that are very important to the building of an empire:

- We must have eye-catching material that's straight forward and to the point.
- Too much information keeps people distracted.
- A potential client that's distracted is a client that may turn away.

- Keep it simple and to the point.
- Most people do not like to read and they will only read to the extent of a glance.

Try not to waste valuable time redoing things that you have an opportunity to get right the first time around. As you commit to this marketing process, do not waste unnecessary money. Trust me, this process takes time to manifest and develop, so wasting time, energy and money is not an option when it comes down to this phase of the business.

Unique marketing is needed, so we must pray through this process as we keep our eyes and ears open to other ways to market what we are doing. When embarking upon this marketing journey we must make a commitment to patiently persevere through all obstacles. Actually, we must consistently think toward greatness by learning how to market our business strategically. However, we must first know and understand our purpose for doing what we are doing and then find out our target market. Basically, we need to find out who needs what we have to offer. Actually, by knowing this we are then able to create a sense of urgency or hunger for what we are offering.

Constructive knowledge that's applied in the right direction has enough strength to empower us to succeed where we have previously failed. The groundwork for greatness starts with a constructive way of thinking and living that provides a benefit to ourselves and others. The way in which we build ourselves up or tear ourselves down on a daily basis will determine the level of greatness that we will attain. In so many words, what we do with and for ourselves daily governs our ability to become great or destructive in other areas of our lives. A life that falls apart can come back together, and a life that's together can fall apart if we do not evaluate what we are doing or what we are not doing. And, regardless of where we may have failed in life, we can succeed if we leave no stone unturned.

Anything that you are thinking about constructing, building or enhancing, make sure you lay the proper groundwork to ensure that it becomes an asset and not a liability. And, not only that, be very cautious about investing in something or someone that's going to cost you mentally, physically, emotionally, spiritually, or financially more than you are willing to pay.

Our marketing plan lays the foundation for the promotion of our business. We must have an outline of what we are going to do whether we have the money or not. Trust me, we can have the best business plan in the world, but if we lack the ability to market it, then we very well may fall short. Our plan does not have to be long; actually, it's better to keep our plan simple and attainable to ensure that we are able to carry it out. Of course, with experience and perseverance, we are able to update and enhance a simple plan to an outstanding one when the time is right.

It does not matter where we are in the marketing phase of our business—there are a few things that we must know:

1. Know your product and its purpose.
2. Know how you can make a difference.
3. Know your market.
4. Know the impact of what you have to offer.
5. Know your competition.
6. Know how you are going to create the urgency for your product or service.
7. Know how you are going to share the benefits of what you have to generate an income.

Remember, this marketing plan will need to be read six days a week, taking the seventh day to rest. Regardless of whether our seventh day is Saturday or Sunday—we must do it. I know this seems a bit much, but we must master this plan by diligently getting it into our heart; while making adjustments as the market changes, as competition challenges us, as people forget about us and as we try to keep our budgets within the range of what we can afford. We must keep our marketing as inexpensive as possible; this will prevent us from losing out before we really begin. Some things may work and some things may not—it's all about trial and error. So, keep your budgets to a minimum while maximizing all of the things that you can do for free.

# Chapter 2

## The Goals of the Marketing Game

Greatness is not achieved by winging it. Actually, it is achieved by having a system in place to keep us focused on the goal and not the obstacle. Living life is not about who is the most intelligent, it's about who's the most committed and who's the most focused on achieving, doing, and being more than what they are right now. Taking action will help you to overcome the challenges that may easily beset you from achieving your desired result or your desired goal. And, when doing so, you must answer these 3 questions:

1. What are you trying to achieve?

2. What's the main objective of this achievement?

3. How can this achievement provide a benefit to others?

Instead of being mired by defeat, get a plan and stick to it; therefore, winging it will become a thing of the past. Plus, when you know your strengths, weaknesses, skills, values, attitudes, and interests, you will become better prepared for the surprises that life may spring up on you. As you know, if we want to become successful, we must plan for it. It is impossible to have true success without learning how to plan, set and achieve a desired outcome. In so many words, setting and achieving goals is a prerequisite for SUCCESS. I know that you have your business plan in your head, but it's much better to have it on paper as well. As a matter of fact, having your business plan written down on paper will help you stay on track more than just having it in your head.

I often get the question, "Why are you marketing you?" And, my answer has always been that there is no one who can market me better than me, and no one will work as hard as I would. As a matter of fact, I know the vision better than anyone else, and I know where my heart is. So, it is my responsibility to pick up the torch and run with it. I am able to serve me better than anyone else. Yes, I am a celebrity, but I am a servant first—I am here to serve others. No matter how small your business is, you need to establish and position your brand. Your brand communicates what you do, how you do it and what sets you apart from competitors.

Most often, we get excited about the appearance of success; however, we cannot allow ourselves to become deceive by material gain. My friend, material gain is a great perk and added benefit; but, if we haven't a clue how we attained it, how to keep it and how to manage it—it will find itself some wings and fly away or we will never become satisfied with it, creating a void from within.

Very few people set goals, so that means that there are a lot of people who are not accomplishing what they set out to accomplish. And, our level of achievement is definitely related to how we progress through life, whether it is aimlessly, effortlessly, diligently, or strategically. Now, my question is, "Would you travel to another state without a map or GPS system?" The chance of us traveling without some form of guidance is very slim. So, why are we living our lives or running a business without some form of guideline? We think just because we have the goal in our head, that's good enough; however, I beg to differ on that one. Our mind changes so often that we fail to keep up with it; therefore, making it imperative to write our goals out.

When we become clear about what we want, our lives will start attracting the people, places and things to make it happen. Furthermore, true success is established when we are able to set and achieve the goals or the desires of our heart. Therefore, making it imperative for us to think, prepare and commit to ourselves as well as our goals, ideas or desires. And, by doing so, our goals become easier for us, we are able to explain our goals to others and it makes our goals seemingly permanent, while keeping us more committed.

The key to accomplishing what we want is to learn how to plan our lives in a backward motion. When we plan our lives backward, we are better able to determine the steps needed to get to our desired destination. Therefore, giving us better control of our ability to focus on what we want oppose to what we don't want. When we focus on what we don't want, we become fearful and we give up before we get started. Plus, we must have an idea of where we want to go or what we want to achieve in life, in order to better govern our destiny. And, if you do not have a clue about what I am talking about, here are some tips:

- *Know and understand your values to ensure that your goals are going to line up with what you believe.* It's not in your best interest to have conflicted beliefs and values working against the goal that you have set for yourself. So, your best bet is to keep your goal positive.

- *Put it in writing.* You must get your goals on paper because it will provide a road map for you. You must activate the power of your written word.

- *Be specific.* Write down exactly what you want without being evasive. Answer the what, when, where, how and why's of the goal, what you want or what you desire. In so many words, here is where you describe your goals in detail.

- *Know and understand your objective.* It's the reason behind your goal. You must know why you set the goal, why you want to achieve the goal, and why it's important to you.

- *Know the benefit.* We are creatures of habit and we gravitate to pleasure oppose to pain. And, for that reason, you must know how this goal is going to benefit you and your life. If there isn't a benefit, then more than likely you will not stick to the goal.

- *Know why this goal is important to you.* You must know the value of your goals. Rest assured that the people, places, and things that you do not find value in, you will lose interest in them.

- *Know what type of impact it's going to have on your life.* Anything worth having, you are going to sacrifice something, and it's up to you to know what that something is.

- *Keep your goals simple but not easy.* Life is not hard; therefore, goals are not hard—it is our power of choice or being pushed out of our comfort zone that becomes difficult. In so many words, our thoughts are really what keep things complicated in our lives. However, the more you become accustom to setting and achieving your goals, you will become a pro at it.

- *Think about your goals thoroughly and visualize them.* We are very visual! If you cannot see mentally what you believe, then more than likely you will not get it. It's important to be able to see mentally what you desire to bring into reality.

- *Make a plan on how you are going to get one step closer to your goal every day.*

- *Keep yourself organized.* Clutter cause distractions mentally; therefore, affecting the flow of your process of thought.

- *Read your goals 6 days a week and take 1 day off.* It's imperative that you read your goals over and over—this will definitely help keep you on track. This is actually adjusting your thoughts to accommodate what you desire from your goal, passion, or dream.

- *Pray about it.* This keeps you sincere and it keeps you on the right road, even if you come to some form of crossroad in your life. You must know that God is your Source that will provide the resources necessary to accomplish your goal, passion or dream.

- *Keep your goals achievable*—take one step at a time to ensure that you do not become overwhelmed.

- *Align yourself in the environment of your goal.*

- *Get a support group, mentor or coach.* Support from others keeps you more committed to your goal. It's easy to hide the accomplishment of a goal if it's kept a secret; but if your goal is made known to others, you are not going to give up as easy. Plus, it's always good to have a coach or mentor.

- *Maximize all of our resources.* A goal is not set in stone; therefore, we don't know which stone will provide an added benefit. And, for that reason we must not leave any stone unturned when working toward a goal. We must utilize all of our resources.

- *Focus on the goal and not your past failures or mishaps.* Keep a positive mindset at all times. Keep an accurate evaluation of where you are or how close you are to your goal.

- *Set a deadline or timeline for yourself.* This will better help you get to your desired destination in a timely manner.

- *Now, it's time to take action.* If you fail at taking action one day, take action the next day without giving up on yourself.

- *We must keep an open mind to ensure that we are able to recognize opportunity* when it presents itself in our life without becoming obsessed with it.

- *Journal every day.* This will help you keep track of what you are doing, and the reasons why. Don't forget to journal about your:

| | |
|---|---|
| Career | Health |
| Family | Spiritual Life |
| Friends | Mental Status |
| Finances | Dreams |

If you are at a loss about what you desire, ask yourself 3 questions to get a jumpstart on designing the rest of your life:

1. If you could do anything, what would you do?
2. If you could become anything, what would it be?
3. If you could accomplish anything, what would you accomplish?

Answer those questions honestly and you will be well on your way to setting and achieving the desires of your heart.

Listed below is a sample goal template that will help you set your personal goals:

## Mentally:

_____

_____

_____

_____

**Action:**

_____

_____

_____

**Start date:** _____ **Deadline date:** _____

# Physically:

_____

_____

_____

_____

_____

_____

## Action:

_____

_____

_____

_____

**Start date:** _____ **Deadline date:** _____

# Emotionally:

_____

_____

_____

_____

_____

_____

## Action:

_____

_____

_____

_____

**Start date:** _____ **Deadline date:** _____

# Spiritual:

_____

_____

_____

_____

_____

## Action:

_____

_____

_____

_____

**Start date:** _____ **Deadline date:** _____

# Financially:

_____

_____

_____

_____

_____

_____

## Action:

_____

_____

_____

_____

**Start date:** _____ **Deadline date:** _____

# Socially:

_____

_____

_____

_____

_____

## Action:

_____

_____

_____

_____

**Start date:** _____ **Deadline date:** _____

# Family matters:

_____

_____

_____

_____

_____

_____

## Action:

_____

_____

_____

_____

**Start date:** _____ **Deadline date:** _____

# Health:

_____

_____

_____

_____

_____

_____

## Action:

_____

_____

_____

_____

**Start date:** _____ **Deadline date:** _____

# Business:

_____

_____

_____

_____

_____

## Action:

_____

_____

_____

_____

**Start date:** _____ **Deadline date:** _____

# Marketing:

_____

_____

_____

_____

_____

_____

## Action:

_____

_____

_____

_____

**Start date:** _____ **Deadline date:** _____

# Chapter 3
## Selling Yourself

Drifting aimlessly away from our goals is commonly the reason we create excuses not to do what needs to be done. Excuses, excuses, excuses—we all have them. When we don't want to do something, we make an excuse. When we don't want to go somewhere, we make an excuse. When we don't want to think about something, we make an excuse. When we are late, we make an excuse. When we get caught in a lie, we make an excuse. When we get caught in our folly, we make an excuse. If you haven't made an excuse, just live a little longer and you will eventually make one.

Some people live their lives making excuses for not doing, some people make excuses for not living and some people make excuses to live. Regardless of the excuse, it does not negate the fact that we must accept responsibility for our actions, reactions, commitments and the lack thereof. When we become lazy mentally, we often cover it up by uneventful excuses that drive us away from our goal or commitments. However, you must find a way to center your action on the goal and not the excuse. If you are in it to win it, you will find that you will start making progress in the right direction until you cross the finish line of ultimate success. From me to you, if you are going to make an excuse—make an excuse to succeed!

The neediness of those who refuse to help themselves will fall prey to the victim mentality, unless they strive a little harder to stand up on their own two feet. The best thing that we can ever do for ourselves is to stand up on our own. When we become too needy, we will find that people will start to pull away from us to seek their own space. And, for that reason, we must become mindful of our wants and needs to ensure that we are not placing any false expectations on people, places and things that are not obligated to fulfill our needs anyway.

We will find that needy people do desperate things. And, our neediness is one of the factors that cause us to become desperate—desperate for love, desperate for attention, desperate for conversation, or desperate for whatever; which will hinder the way in which we do business! Furthermore, the sense of desperation is a repellant and it really causes people to run from each other; for example, men run from desperate women and women run from desperate men and if we don't run—we should! When we conquer the sense of our desperation or neediness, we will then start to develop our own sense of independence or interdependence. And, getting what you want is not hard, as long as you KNOW what you don't need. Stop wasting time on people, places and things that are not positive and productive. You are not getting any younger—life is too short to keep picking up things that keep you distracted and stressed out. Trust God for the big things as well as the simple things to ensure that you enjoy your life and maximize your true potential without appearing desperate, needy or doubtful.

Saturated doubt has a way of supporting the failures of those who are not willing to create stepping-stones out of their mishaps in life. A crystal clear perspective about our mishaps and setbacks in life leaves little room for doubt. And, having a perspective about our lives does not mean that we have all the answers. What it means is that we are able to trust life to create a magnetic force of our beliefs. For example, if you believe that everything happens for a reason—then life will avail itself to reveal the reason to you. Now, whether you believe that reason is a stepping-stone or a set-back is totally up to you.

When our perspective is foggy, it has a way of preventing us from clearly envisioning the desires of our heart. In so many words, we become confused or doubtful about our wants and needs in life; therefore, settling for temporary comfort that ends in the appearance of a set-back or failure. As simple as it may seem, it is extremely hard for others to understand and relate to us, when we don't understand how to relate to ourselves effectively. Often enough, it's in our nature to want people to understand our wants, needs and desires; but, if we lack the understanding of our own wants, needs and desires, then we set ourselves up for our own disappointment. My friend, know and understand what you want, need and desire in life and out of life, leaving little or no room for doubt to have its way in your life.

Get rid of the inferiority complex. Never allow the thoughts of you not being good enough, thoughts of you not being an expert or the thought of you not being famous enough to hold you back from succeeding. Of course, there very well maybe someone better than you, but who cares? If you are dealing with this inferiority complex—open and honestly ask yourself and answer these questions:

1. Who am I?

2. Why am I here?

3. What is my purpose in life?

4. What do I really want out of life?

5. What are my strengths?

6. What are my weaknesses?

7. What am I afraid of? Why?

8. What are my values?

9. What are my priorities?

10. What motivates me?

11. What discourages me?

12. What makes me happy?

13. What makes me sad?

14. Am I honest with myself?

15. Who do I need to forgive? Why?

16. What type of effect do I have on others?

17. What opportunities do I have available to me?

18. What steps should I take to get what I want?

19. How can I improve the quality of my life?

20. Are there any real roadblocks on my path? Why?

21. What do I need to change about me in order to grow?

22. What are my responsibilities?

23. Am I willing to live a fulfilled life of integrity?

24. Are you willing to brand yourself?

25. What will be the difference in your branding?

26. What is the desired outcome for your brand?


You are the brand that leaves a positive or negative stamp on a person's heart. Of course, you want that brand to be positive, because people talk more about a negative experience than they would a positive one; therefore, making it extremely important to hone in on good customer service to compliment your product or service. Remember, there is always 3 sides to every story—your side, the other person's side and the truth. When making decisions, we must evaluate all three; if not, we will find ourselves making permanent decisions on one-sided information.

It is imperative to look at things from a different perspective. This will definitely help us in the decision making process to ensure that we are making the best and the wisest decisions based on the information that we have in front of us. Now with that being said, why do we often hold on to people, places and things that are not working or entertaining people, places and things that are counterproductive? We can say that it's fear, we can say that it's guilt, we can say that it's out of obligation, we can say that it's a lot of things; but, the truth is that most often we settle because we don't want to ask questions or we only get half of the story. Now, in order to get the proper feedback, we must ask open-ended questions, eliminating the "yes" or "no" answers.

Making decisions without having the facts presented to us will eventually cause us to make unnecessary mistakes. Yes, we are able to learn from our mistakes; however, some mistakes can be avoided by taking a moment to think through and ask questions about our decision making process. My friend, it's good to ask questions. It's okay to know the details when it comes down to you, your well-being and your business. Always remember, most bad decisions are derived out of impatience or the lack of information. From now on, take a little more time to get the facts!

Through *"Millionaire Hustle,"* I show individuals how to take their ashes and make them profitable through self-analysis and goal setting. We cannot lose with having success God's way. Your brand is basically your simplified strategy on how to grow and develop your business to leave a lasting impression. This is accomplished through a diversified objective. You'll need to define a strategy for growing your business. When we are clear about what we want, how we want it, and how we are going to get there, our sense of direction will then take its rightful place in helping you build a good, sound and conducive network of people. Rationalizing and justifying our attitude, actions, reactions and responses will cause us to sell ourselves short when we are designed to sell ourselves high. The best ways to market your product or service is through:

1. Your Website
2. Business Cards
3. Newsletters
4. Email Campaigns
5. Banners
6. Writing Articles
7. Press Releases
8. Becoming an expert
9. Blogging
10. Social Networking

11. Viral Networking
12. Attending Community Events
13. Word of mouth

Now, the question is, "Who is going to buy our product or service?" We must know and understand who wants our product or service, why they want it and what you can do to keep them buying from you. The first step is to learn how to buy ourselves first. If we don't buy ourselves, then who will? It's amazing; but, we are the sellers and the buyers of ourselves before a product or service can be effectively sold. Trust me, when it comes down to us, it will always be a buyer's and a seller's market simultaneously. My friend, people don't buy us because for some odd reason, we may not be buying ourselves. Most people dislike selling as much as they dislike sells people, without realizing that we sell and promote ourselves every time we open our mouth, with every move that we make, etc. Regardless of how we try to rationalize and justify it, we all sell ourselves in some way, shape or form making everyone a sales person whether we like it or not.

So, if you are not getting what you want, simply check or adjust what you are doing and why you are doing it. My friend, the quality of your product is revealed by your attitude, actions, reactions and responses. Today, take the time to choose your words carefully—you never want to sell yourself short when you are quality at its best. And, there is no reason why you should not be able to succeed at what you do best.

## Find the Problem and Solve it

We must find a way to solve a problem. The way to excel in what we do, we must give people what they want and they will give us what we want. In so many words, we must provide some sort of solution to a problem. When we make the lives of others easier, then our life will become easier as well. A product such as ourselves, an idea, an item or service has no value until it is SOLD. When we find our purpose for selling or sharing what we have, we will then be able to master our unique niche. Our niche will definitely work in our favor as long as we follow the proper order of divine protocol or code of proper behavior.

The internet has become a viable resource for us to market ourselves with little or no money. However, we must find the most sensible and the most cost effective way to do so.

**Know who and what you are selling**

We must be able to buy ourselves first. If you do not buy you, then what make you think that others will buy what you are offering? That's not possible. We must find a way to believe in what we are selling; if not, people will know or sense it and they will not buy. People buy YOU! Most often, we don't want to admit it but it's the truth. If we are flaky in our presentation, we will become flaky in asking for the money.

There is no reason to fast-talk or deceive others when marketing something that you believe in. When you have a product or service that you believe in:

1. You don't mind sharing the information.
2. You will find a way to network with people who are in your field or who wants what you have to offer.

3. You are able to keep them interested in what you have.
4. You will become excited about what you are doing or selling.
5. You will be able to ask for the money without feeling guilty.
6. You will be able to ask for referrals. If they cannot take advantage of what you have to offer, they may know someone else who could benefit from your product or service.
7. You don't mind receiving feedback to ensure that you are able to become better at doing business.
8. You don't mind using your company name and logo on everything; especially your personal or private emails.

# Chapter 4
## Keep a Clear Mind When Selling

If whatever you want out of life will be, then it's left up to you to take the initiative to do what you need to do with a clear mind! You are in control over your emotions, actions, reactions, thoughts, intents, your vocabulary and the direction of your life.

Now, my question is, "How bad do you want to market your dream?" When we start walking in our dream, talking about our dream, and breathing our dream—then we know we got it bad! Most often, it is when we are so close to having the desires of our heart that we give up. Giving up too soon or not trying at all has and will hinder those who become stagnate in their way of thinking. When we want something out of life, sitting on the couch day in and day out, is not going to get it. We must get up out of our comfort zone and do something about the situation or circumstance we are in without expecting others to do it for us. If you are waiting for someone to believe in you—stop waiting. It starts with you believing in you. As a matter of fact, no one can truly believe in you better than you can. You have what you have, work with it. You are who you are, work with it. It is what it is, work with it. There is no need to beat yourself up about people, places and things that you cannot change. Work with what you have to get the results that you want, and most often, your break-through is usually right under your nose.

When we are promoting ourselves, we must keep a clear mind. We cannot focus on our problems when we are providing a solution to others. This counteracts our ability to focus on the prospect and their needs. Remember, if we listen effectively, people will tell us what they need, what they want and how to sell them the solution. And, with that being said, meditate to bring your heart and mind to a place of peace before you present whatever you have to others.

In order to gain control over our lives and to market effectively, we must find a way to plan our day to control our time. Of course, creating a to-do list will help; but there is much more to time management. We must also have a *not to-do list* to better govern our time. This will help to ensure that our time is not wasted on unproductive or unfruitful people, places and things that may disrupt our set of core values. Of course, there will be some things that we cannot control; but for the most part, we need to become a good steward over the time in which we do have. In order to gain control over our life we must:

***Prioritize what we do, say, think and become.*** We must know and understand the reason behind what we are doing. Doing something "just because" is no longer an option. Once we learn the "what's and why's" behind what we are doing, then we are better able to spend our time wisely without bringing about neglect, chaos and confusion.

***Do the most important things FIRST.*** Make a list of things you need to do, based on the time of day in which you need to do them. Start with the MOST IMPORTANT and do that first, then proceeding on to the other things on your list. This will help you better determine the value of what you are doing; which will cause you to become more productive in the things that you need to accomplish. This helps eliminate the temptation of procrastination.

***Learn how to say "NO."*** Saying "NO" to unproductive, unbeneficial or unfruitful people, places and things is a great way to say "Yes" to discipline. As we all know, there is a time and a place for everything. And, creating extra work for ourselves is not an option when we have enough or when we are not able to complete what we already have. Furthermore, unfinished projects can and will cause our goals, priorities and schedule to shift in a direction that we may or may not like.

***It's your right to delegate.*** We cannot do everything on our own; we all need a little help every now and then. This is not about getting rid of the things that we don't want to do—it's about delegating to those who are able to complete tasks that we are willing to do, but lack the time to do so.

*Focus on quality over quantity.* Doing quality work will supersede doing a poor job any day. However, when it takes more time to redo what should have already been completed—takes up more time than doing it right from the beginning. Of course, we will all make mistakes, but if our mistakes are costing us, then we need to reevaluate what we are doing and why we are doing it. Doing everything in the spirit of excellence is better than doing something "just because."

*A little goes a long way.* If we have a big project that seems overwhelming, simply breakup the project into smaller tasks to ensure that we do not become burned out. For example, most of us dread working-out for 40 minutes a day; but if we split our workout into 4 increments of 10 minutes; 10 minutes in the morning, 10 minutes at break-time, 10 minutes after lunch and a 10 minute workout before bed—guess what? We have out 40 minute workout without having the dread of it.

*Keep track of time.* The value of our time will elude us if we don't find a way to keep track of it or our accomplishments for the day. Journal the time that's spent as well as the little small blessings that keeps us on our toes. This will ensure that we are able to get back on track when we get off track.

**Set a deadline.** Carve out a certain amount of time to complete a project. For example, instead of taking all day to answer emails, schedule a deadline of 30-90 minute increments to answer emails. The key is not to allow things to pile up—this will definitely cut down on wasted time.

**Focus without undue or unjustified distractions.** Set aside a certain time of day that you cannot have any distractions, PERIOD. This time can be used for prayer, call-backs, reading emails, paying bills, etc. This is the time that you have in your day that is dedicated to a certain task(s). This will enable you to keep you focus in the midst of your busyness.

**Find a system that works for you.** Having a system creates productivity. However, don't get so caught up in one way of doing something to the point where you are unwilling to adjust a system that's not working or a system that needs adjusting.

***Take time to relax.*** The best way to release stress is to relax. When we are stressed out, it reduces our effort to become or stay organized. Take time out to take care of YOU, besides you deserve it.

These are just a few ways to jumpstart your time management skills.

# Chapter 5

## The Value of Sharing

The haphazard way of living has a way of keeping us questioning life, when life is here to provide the answers. What is life trying to tell you? Or, better yet, what is that little nudge inside of you saying? If you don't know or don't care, you will find that history will constantly repeat itself in your life. Unwise decisions have a way of causing us to spin our wheels getting nowhere. Living our lives without a guideline will cause us to become easily frustrated, confused, and lackadaisical. There are times when we don't have a clue about what we want, what we are doing or the reason why. Therefore, we begin to settle for whatever, expecting life to give us something or someone that provides a temporary comfort.

In order to better plan your day, you must know what it will consist of or at least have an idea. Living everyday "just because" is totally unacceptable when you have the ability to govern most things that happen in your life and how it will affect you. As a matter of fact, when you find the answer to your purpose, you are better able to ignite the passion that you have hidden within you. Successful people are doing this day in and day out, and so can you—simply start writing out your goals, action plans, and time frames! Your wealth is in that purposeful passion that resides from within. Find it, use it and share it with someone else.

It is your responsibility to share information and not tell; you must present yourself as an expert. Blog as an expert, speak as an expert, help others as an expert, target your market like an expert, build your network like an expert, nurture relationships like an expert and live your life like an expert who don't mind learning more to polish up his or her expertise. Plus, you are better able to up-sale your product or service when people find value in it.

We can get more out of people when we simply share information. People do not like to be told what to do—they will resist what you are presenting if you become too bossy. Bossy sellers are the sellers that turnover quickly—these are considered the fast talkers. However, they do bring in the sales; but, they will also find that their prospect will end up with buyer's remorse; therefore canceling or returning the item. When we develop a relationship sale, people are less likely to have buyer's remorse because they have an understanding of what they have purchased. When we share information, we actually help them to think through the process and not think about the process. There is a big difference between the two because when we think about something too long—it leaves room for error or justification, which can go both ways. We must fine-tune the presentation of what we have to cover the objections in the sharing process. When we knock out the objections ahead of time, we then are able to build a buying relationship to close a solid sale that will end up in them sending you more prospects.

When we place value in the true essence of our gratefulness, we will then open ourselves up to the invincible nuggets of wisdom. There are hidden messages of wisdom that's wrapped up in everyday living. My friend, every day is designed to teach us something, every day is designed to give us something and every day is designed to take something away. Regardless, of how we see life—life is doing what it's designed to do. And, sometimes, life has a way of asking us, "What are we doing with our life?" Or, it may ask us, "Are we doing what we are designed to do?" When we become grateful where we are, we will better understand where we are going and we are better able to share it as well. As a matter of fact, it is our awareness of truth that provokes the inner wisdom from within. When we lie and deceive ourselves, we will find that wisdom will evade us in that particular area of our life. So, if you need to work on something, work on it. If you need to do something, do it. If you need to say something, say it.

The desire to win compiled with a little discipline and self-control will keep our emotions from running on high; especially, when making wise decisions. Wisdom is priceless. Today, don't run from wisdom, run toward it and watch the door of understanding swing wide open so that you are able to share it.

# Chapter 6
## Cultivating your Social Network

Our competency and credibility are both fueled by our ability to enhance our people skills; therefore, creating a magnetism that stands out. If we want to enhance our people skills, we must find a way to allow our inner charisma to create a personal magnet. My friend, a charismatic person stands out, even when no one is looking. As a matter of fact, a charismatic person has an appeal that sends out silent messages that prompt people to flock to them.

When we place our attention, positively in the right direction, we then allow life to serve us. In spite of what's going on in our life, our demeanor says more than we care to imagine. We evaluate people by the silent messages that they send out regardless of whether we understand them or not. Eye contact, for example, builds rapport that sends out a signal of trust or the lack thereof; and not only that, eye contact will send out a silent message of a connection or a repellant. When we leave ourselves unchecked and insensitive to others, we will find ourselves wearing people down that we should be building up. When we drain others, rest assured that people will soon start draining us. However, we have control over this process whether we realize it or not. If we simply choose to treat people right, regardless of what they do, say or become—we then give our credibility enough room to create a personal magnet that has a hidden appeal of greatness.

How often do we show appreciation to the people, places and things around us? If we really take a look within ourselves, we will find that we sometimes forget to say "Thank-you" or "I appreciate you" quite often. Furthermore, the lack of appreciation will cause the best of us to feel like a victim or feel as if we are being used; therefore, causing our natural defense system to kick into high gear. Of course, our ego contributes to some form of selfishness; however, it does not supersede the power of a simple "Thank-you" or "I appreciate you." Saying it, is just as important as showing it; regardless of whether we feel as if it is deserved or not. Appreciation is not bought, it is given—buying our way through life will only get us so far. As a matter of fact, we will never see appreciation packaged on a shelf; but, we are able to give something as a token of our appreciation. None the less, when it comes down to true appreciation—we cannot put a price tag on it.

My friend, let nothing take the place of a simple "Thank-you" or "I appreciate you." And, if you want to be appreciated, simply give appreciation with no strings attached. We must understand that people really build our business. We need people and people need us, according to the cycle of life. And, without people, what do we have? Nothing, right? People talk, whether we want them to or not. When we share, people tell. People have influence over others and they tell people what they need. This is reality, and if they like you—they will tell at least 9 other people about you. However, this cycle can and will work either positively or negatively; so we must find a way to keep it on the positive end of the scale to produce the results that we truly desire. Furthermore, when cultivating your social network, they do not like to be sold, they like to be nurtured. They will support you if you do not make them feel as if it's all about selling them what you have. Of course, you must lay the ground work for the sale, but you must never become pushy or overbearing to get them to purchase your product or service. When you treat your network like royalty, they will buy from you and they will convince others to buy from you as well. We must plant a seed of what we have to offer, give it some time and the harvest will come as long as we are patient.

When publically building your social network, join and attend your local clubs, forums, committees and organizations. Effective networking does require for you to be seen—you must become active in your local organizations to ensure that it's worth your time. As you begin to recognize more people, your network will become larger with added referrals. Word of mouth advertising is effective and it's an invaluable business building tool that will help you build a contact list of good, quality leads. Listed below are some tips when networking or socializing publically:

1. Socialize with more than one person. Do not get caught up in a social clique—you must get to know someone new every time you attend a social function.
2. Network with everyone, leaving no stone unturned. Do not become limited to meeting someone with a title; you want to meet someone with connections.
3. Reframe from becoming emotionally engulfed where you are networking. Keep your personal life to yourself—this is not the place to discuss what's going on at home.
4. Dress appropriately for the occasion. Appearance is of the utmost importance.
5. Limit your drinking at all social functions and parties. You never want to risk losing your credibility for having one too many.
6. Be on your best behavior.
7. Exude confidence while remaining approachable. Low self-esteem can be sensed a mile away.
8. Remember names. If at all possible, never tell a person that you don't remember his or her name.

9. Arrive early with business cards in hand; therefore, you are able to meet more prospects.
10. Take a small note pad and pen with you. Write small details about a prospect and attach it to their business card to ensure that you are able to remember certain things about them.
11. Introduce yourself with a handshake.
12. Always pick up your own tab. Never expect anyone to pay your bills. The reason why you are networking is to ensure that you are able to hold your own.

When cultivating your social network, you must build a relationship with your team, your mentor and your network. Even though, we are dealing with our team, our mentor or our network of friends, we must never make them feel as if they are engaging in a conditional friendship. Conditional friendships works as a repellant to those who will gracefully help people who are genuine—acting FAKE is not going to get us to the penthouse of substance. Besides, it is extremely difficult to maximize our full potential without having a network of people to support us and what we are doing. It's going to take a great network of people, coupled with passion, integrity and sincerity to get us to the top and keep us there.

Internet marketing is now one of the quickest ways to build a social network. However, you must constantly enhance your knowledge and skills particularly with regards to what's new on the internet. It's imperative that you learn how to maximize the online social media network to promote your business. However, you must learn how to do things for yourself on the internet to ensure that you do not have to spend extra money paying for that in which you can do for yourself. Listed below are social media websites where you are able to promote your business:

1. www.FaceBook.com
2. www.plus.google.com
3. www.Intagram.com
4. www.disqus.com
5. www.Pinterest.com
6. www.Twitter.com
7. www.MySpace.com
8. www.Plaxo.com

9. www.Digg.com
10. www.LinkedIn.com
11. www.Xing.com
12. www.Livespaces.com
13. www.Groupsites.com
14. www.SavortheSuccess.com
15. www.Blogtalkradio.com
16. www.youtube.com
17. www.stumbleupon.com
18. www.snapchat.com
19. www.whatsapp.com

You will be surprised about how quickly you can build your network through these particular social connections. Just remember, the more you know about people or your prospects, the more apt they are to buy what you have to offer. It's okay to keep your own personal notes on your friends, family, co-workers, boss, client, associate, etc. Or, better yet, keep a contact database with names, phone numbers, addresses, occupation, birthdays, name of spouse and children. This will help you remember the little small details that mean a lot to people. Plus, it gives you an opportunity to send them cards, gifts or flowers for a birthday, holiday or special occasion. This is one marketing tool that will woo your clients.

# Chapter 7

## Keep it Positive at All Cost

The essence of our communication, body language and attitude are critical non-verbal elements needed to help us get what we want, convey what we don't want and to better govern our approach to our clients or customers. Now, my question is, "How is your approach?" Are you demanding, too shy, arrogant, egotistical, pushy, overbearing, or smoooooth with your approach. Believe it or not, a simple well thought-out approach tends to be the most effective way of getting what you want or getting rid of what you don't want. Becoming aware of our approach is definitely a plus when someone has something that we desire or need their help in attaining. Whether it's corporate survival, board-room survival, home survival or relationship survival, we must pay attention to the way in which we are silently communicating. We need people and people need us. And, regardless of how insignificant we may or may not feel, we are designed to give and receive help from time-to-time. We are just as responsible for giving help as we are for receiving help. Now, with that being said, we also must be very careful on how we approach people. Our approach is usually the determining factor in the level of assistance that we are going to give or receive.

As you very well know, you are not the Lone Ranger when it comes down to living life. People are going to reject what you have, just because they want to reject you. And, this should not change your attitude toward them at all. This is called a practice session for the nay sayers—so what if they don't want what you have to offer, keep it positive and don't waste too much time trying to convince them. It is not necessary to convince someone who has his or her mind made up. Don't be afraid to move on to someone who will give you an opportunity to share what you have to offer. When you know that you have value in what you are selling or presenting, don't waste it on those who spend time devaluing people, places and things that's providing a good service to those who need it. Today, open yourself up to give and receive help while mastering the essence of the way in which you communicate. And, by doing so, it will amaze you at how the doors of opportunity start to swing wide open.

A winning attitude consists of being patient, kind, sincere and polite. A winning attitude is never rude or demeaning. When we commit to excellence, it is revealed in everything that we do or say. My friend, when all else fails, a winning attitude will not! So, get your press releases started with a winning attitude. In your press release, you must tell people what you are doing and how it's going to benefit them. People buy benefits and not features! What's in it for them is the ultimate question.

The best way to let people know what you are doing is to send out a press release. A press release basically tells people what you are doing, why you are doing it and the benefit. A good press release will consist of:

1. For Immediate Release at the top of the press release.
2. Identify your organization.
3. A contact person with phone, email and address.
4. Date of your release.
5. Give details of Who, What, When, Why and How.
6. Summarize what you are doing in the first two sentences.
7. Always speak in second person.
8. Keep it concise and to the point.
9. Double check your grammar, spelling and typographical errors.
10. Make sure the timing is right.
11. Post your press release on your website as well.

Websites to assist you with your Press Release:
1. www.ideamarketers.com
2. www.openpr.com
3. www.seminarannouncer.com
4. www.internetwire.com
5. www.prweb.com

# Chapter 8
## Make it Fun

We enjoy things that we have fun at. When we are having fun at what we do, we have much less time to become stressed-out over things that may work against us. As a matter of fact, stressed-out people are usually the most worried people. Worrying about our next sale can and will put pressure on us. And, usually when we are under pressure, we overdo it and chase our prospects away. My friend, pressuring people will cause them to inadvertently flee from us. They actually enjoy being around people who enjoy themselves and those who enjoy what they do. The art of successful living is learning how to motivate others through our wisdom, creativity, ambitions or skills without allowing bragging or boasting to clout our results or the lack there of.

Are you boosting yourself up or are you giving someone else a fun boost today? Our wisdom is not just for our use. Our creativity is not just for our enjoyment. Our ambitions are not of our own. Our skills are not just for our pleasure. Everything that we have is designed to encourage or bless the lives of someone else. Of course, we are blessed to bless someone else and this is how it should be. However, when we feel blessed, it's so easy to get caught up in bragging about what we have, do, say and experience, while forgetting about the law of reciprocity (to give and to receive.) My friend, the art of our true success is based upon the biblical principle of seed, time and harvest—we must plant our seeds of blessings in our time of harvest to ensure that our blessings remain.

It's great to have confidence in our time of harvest; however, having confidence without investing into others will set us up for an ultimate disappointment or let down. We are blessed to be a blessing to someone else and not just a blessing to ourselves. It's our responsibility to find a way to motivate someone through our wisdom, creativity, ambitions or skills to ensure that we maximize the law of use. And, it's a shame to allow an unused or misused blessing to fall by the wayside.

Now, do what you need to do and allow your actions to speak for itself. There is no need to convince someone that you possess a certain type of creativity, wisdom, ambition or skill—just do what you do best, help yourself, help others and allow God to do the rest. And, it's just that simple! When you make something fun, people will get excited and they tell other people. This is the best way to get viral marketing to work for you. Viral Marketing is when people pass information along to other people. This is mostly done through:

1. The forwarding of emails.
2. The forwarding of video or audio clips.
3. The forwarding of pictures.

This form of viral marketing usually provokes some form of emotion through:

1. Laughter.
2. Inspiration.
3. Compassion.

## 4. Motivation.

Remember that people buy out of love, greed, the need for self-help, the need for self-improvement, fear, fame, laziness, greed, recognition, power, prestige, anger, to experience something greater than what they have, necessity, to feed an addiction, and they buy to make a difference. We will buy what we don't need to avoid pain or to gain pleasure—so, when you promote, you must make it fun while appearing to solve a problem for them. And, this is the best time to do affiliate marketing as well. Affiliate marketing is basically placing links on your site that your friends, clients or customers can click on to purchase additional products or services from another company; which in turn pays you a commission. This creates multiple streams of income and you would place these links on your website, emails, newsletters, etc. However, make sure that you are not overloading your clients with affiliate marketing—it will make them run from you. Simply, place a few links on your website or in your emails. You can easily sign up for an account through:

1. www.google.com/ads/affiliatenetwork/
2. www.clickbank.com
3. www.cj.com.
4. www.affiliate-program.amazon.com
5. avangate.com
6. ebaypartnernetwork.com
7. shareasale.com
8. flexoffers.com
9. revenuewire.com

Just make sure that your links are applicable to what you are offering. Oh by the way, don't forget, keep it fun and in good taste.

# Chapter 9
## Jumping for What?

Habitual thoughts are designed to become a constructive or a destructive influence that will determine whether we move in a forward or backward motion. When we are at the crossroad of survival, the thoughts that we think determines the real essence of who we are, what we will become, what or whom we attract and which direction we take. Now, my question is, "What are you thinking about all the time?" If we would ask ourselves this one question, it will prevent us from wasting a lot of time backtracking. When we waste time backtracking, we will soon find ourselves in a rat race moving three steps forward and two steps back making life seemingly unbearable. Moving in a backward motion without a strategy will cause the best of us to become resistant to moving forward, even if it's the right thing to do. As a matter of fact, a strategic motion with some faith behind it can move mountains that would not move otherwise. Even if you have to learn a lesson two or three times, you will find that God will not place more on you than you can actually bear. And, with that being said, you can accomplish anything, if you streamline the superficial or irrelevant thoughts that contributes to regression oppose to progression. And, regardless of how it may or may not appear, keep your mind positive and focused in the right direction until your change comes.

Now, jumping over treasure to pick up junk has a way of distorting the value that we have passed up. The value of the dollar can purchase a lot of things, but character is not one of them. When we get caught up in lowering our standards, we will find that it takes a lot more to build our standards back up again and much more than that to rebuild our character. Regardless of whether we deal with standards or character, choosing junk over the treasures in life, reveals that our vision has been distorted in some way. And, it's our responsibility to focus in on our attitude, actions and reactions to ensure that we are able to pinpoint where we have lost our way.

When we become caught up in the issues of life, we tend to let our guards down in hope of receiving attention to fill an unrecognizable void. And, when we fill that void with something other than what we are really missing, we will find ourselves trying to undue things that are already done, doing things that we should have left alone from the beginning or attracting people, places and things that are out of character for us. Furthermore, it's highly impossible to receive or attract the treasures of life if we have too much junk blocking our way.

Most often, your treasure is right under your nose! However, it's up to you whether or not you take the time or the opportunity to get rid of the junk and sift through the dirt to get to what rightfully belongs to you. From me to you, your overlooked treasures will always keep their hidden value whether it's visible to you or not.

The first rule of thumb is not to get our goals mixed up with our purpose. Our purpose gives us the meaning or reason for doing what we do;

however, setting goals will give us something to work toward or give us something to work at. As a matter of fact, we must have some sort of way to measure our progress. And, trust me, when our progress is not measured, we are only as good as our last sale. Our best bet is to continue to learn, enhance or tighten up our game to produce the results that we want. Just keep in mind, we all want to make money and when it becomes our ultimate goal, we tend to lose focus on what we are supposed to be doing. And, that is SHARING INFORMATION to solve a problem!

When sharing information, you must provide an added benefit. Furthermore, you must also think through what you are trying to achieve to ensure that you are able to maximize your website and marketing methods. You very well may have to polish up your skills to include social networking, on-line blogging, and other sites that engage in interactive blogging. Of course, you want to attract new clients; however, you also want to stay in touch with the clients that you may already have.

# Chapter 10
## Clean Slate

Integrity is something that will set apart those who are moochers and those who sincerely help others who are in need. We all have a moocher in our life, whether we want them to be there or not. The lifestyle of a moocher can go undetected for some time, especially when we have a natural tendency to give and help others. However, a moocher is a person who goes overboard with asking others for help without taking the initiative to do things for themselves. We will often find that the moochers in our lives are really designed to keep us on our toes when we have a tendency to have a hard time saying, "NO." The use of our better judgment will sometimes put us at risk of seemingly being the bad person; but, when we really understand the value of saying "NO"—we put ourselves in a position not to be pressured to say, "YES." Furthermore, saying "YES" to things that we should be saying "NO" to, may eventually put us in a compromising situation later on down the line.

Regardless of whether you are the moocher or the moochee, there is no such thing as a free ride and if you are getting a free ride right now—it will not last long (people will get tired of you or you will get tired of them!) Either way, losing family, friends, or a job over the inability to handle your own weight is totally unacceptable. Living by the principle of "integrity first and stuff later" will take you a lot further than the appearance of a free ride will ever take you. Trust me, when you have your own and pay for your own, you will find that you are better able to look toward God as your source and once you do that, people will do things for you naturally, "Just Because."

Get rid of the clutter in your house, your business, in your advertising and in your marketing plan. However, we are just going to deal with marketing for now. If you haven't noticed, most people only scan advertisements and too much information will cause them to overlook your ad. And, for that reason, you must grab a potential client or prospects attention with an attention-getter headline within 3-5 seconds and anything longer than 15 seconds will put you at risk of losing that client. The most effective attention-getter is a question—when you ask the right question to provoke an interest, they will give you up to 15 seconds to convince them or they will move on.

An organized marketing presentation or an organized sale will reveal a lot about those who are willing to take care of their customer. If we are not organized or consistent in what we are doing, it leaves room for unanswered questions like: Can I trust him or her to get what I need? Can I depend on him or her to take care of the paperwork properly? Can I depend on him or her to follow-up with me? These are indeed relevant questions to ask when we see a mess prior to the sales or presentation process. An unprepared presentation is usually the one that will leave room for doubt and where there is doubt, people will tend to do without. Clean up and organize everything around you to ensure that you do not lose the trust of a sale before you ask for it.

It's imperative that you attract their attention, get them interested, create a burning desire for what you have to offer and create a demand for action. For sure, this method of marketing has sold you time in and time out—just pay attention.

The basic pattern of our normalcy is determined by our attitude, actions and reactions to abnormal people, places and things. What's considered normal for one person could be abnormal for the next. In so many words, our normal is the next persons abnormal or vice-versa. To each his own, when it comes down to what's normal and what's not. However, our normal is determined by our habitual patterns and knowing the difference between what we are doing and saying is as valuable as knowing our name. Our attitudinal intent is basically what transforms our positive actions or reactions into negative ones or vice-versa.

Withdrawing from life is a quick way to become a hermit to people, places and things that we love the most. We cannot escape, disconnect or run from living life—it will catch up with us, because it is designed to do so! No matter how difficult it may seem, life is livable. And, regardless of what's normal and what's not, yelling, screaming, fussing and fighting are totally unacceptable! Furthermore, this type of behavior is not going to solve a problem or resolve an issue; actually, it is this type of behavior that adds fuel to the fire. Negative behavior should never become an excuse for having our way when doing what's right is only a choice away.

Systematic strategies are created to align that which has little or no order. What do we do when our life seems as if it's a MESS? Having a mess will sometimes provoke us to clean up our lives or bring order into our lives to prevent the same thing from happening again. Furthermore, living a chaotic lifestyle is definitely a lifestyle that would benefit from having a system in place. And, in order to better understand the people, places and things that are working for us or working against us, it's imperative that we know and understand the plan of direction that we have set for our own lives. Therefore, giving us an opportunity to adapt and survive through a situation, circumstance or event that has been designed to knock us off our feet.

A systematic plan will always take you further than a clueless or skeptical one. Find your niche, get you a system and work it. My friend, the power of being who you are is often recognized when you are not ashamed to positively believe in yourself without accepting the normalcy of any type of defeat. Today, give yourself permission to take a negative and turn it into something positive

# Chapter 11

## Movers and Shakers

Movers & shakers learn the essence of shaking free of their pride to make a moving impact on the lives of others. Making an impact and getting results is basically what moving and shaking is all about. We are designed to move and when we stop moving or making ourselves better, we become stagnant—stagnant in our thoughts, actions, reactions and the list goes on. When we move and shake the right things, we will find that we attract better results; however, when we move and shake the wrong things, guess what? Our results are not so great. And for that reason, we must find a way to do everything in the spirit of excellence, while putting our pride on the back burner to maximize our effectiveness.

Whether we realize it or not, whatever we touch, our fingerprint is somehow left behind and everyplace that we go, we leave our footprint behind as well. And, whatever we do, say or become can and will leave a positive or negative imprint that may last a lifetime. When we make a positive impact, we then put ourselves in a position to do what we do well, while loving every move, shake, bounce and tumble along the way. My friend, whatever you do, make your impression count for something—you will be amazed at how one word or one act of kindness can change a person's life within a matter of seconds. Just say one word to encourage someone or do one thing to help someone and trust me, it will make you feel good about doing so. You cannot lose, leaving a positive impression on someone's heart. Sale or no sale, marketing or no marketing, everyone wants to be treated with respect.

When we treat everyone great, the law of reciprocity will kick in to grant us greatness in that particular area of our life. When we find something good about someone or something, grace is granted to us whether we realize it or not. These are the brownie points that we definitely do not want to lose. Oh by the way, this will put the icing on the cake when it comes down to us understanding the purpose behind the sale. In so many words, we are relational beings, and when we are able to relate to others effectively, it will definitely propel us in an area that most people fall short. When you treat everyone with respect, they will give you at least 30 seconds to tell them why they should buy you or your product. Therefore, you must have a powerful and persuasive introduction; if not, you may have to overwork yourself for the sale while risking the appearance of desperation.

Inspired commitment has more power than demanding a commitment from those who are designed to have a free-will. Putting people in a box is one of the quickest ways to bring about rebellion in your marketing plan, your environment and on the job. We are designed to soar freely, so we must be able to freely give of ourselves without being forced to do so. We must also recognize the needs of others in order to better fulfill our own needs.

And, for that reason, we must find a way to effectively communicate without confrontation.

Furthermore, when people feel as if they are confronted, they will rebel or shut-down and these are the two things that we must avoid at all cost. I have found that if we want to communicate with others about our wants and needs, we must find a way to speak that other person's language or we may not get in.

When we share, take action and encourage ourselves and others, we then open up the box to allow the true essence of who we are to come out without others taking offense. We do not have to make others feel obligated to us, when they will do it naturally if we give them the room to do so.

# Chapter 12

## Stay on top of your game.

"Success is not accidental, it is skilladental—just know that skilladental savvy will take us much further than accidental savvy ever will. And, it will help you stay on top of your game. I know that I am creating my own word, SKILLADENTAL. However, we need skills if we want to succeed. I always say that your success is not going to come by accident; it's going to come by skill. There is something inside of you that you can do better than anyone else. There is a passion that's inside of you that only you can reckon with. There is greatness that's inside of you that only you can release.

Now, in order to release success from within, you must set goals and take action with diligence. Living our lives with a goal without taking action will cause us to become frustrated with life, enabling us to use everything and everyone as an excuse why we are not taking action. When polishing up our skills, it's imperative that we become interdependent to insure that we are availing ourselves to interdevelopment. That means that we are able to work together with others as a team to develop ourselves to the next level of our creativity. Thinking positive is the first characteristic that will help us to maximize our skills. However, we must know and understand our challenges or limits to ensure that we are able to design an action plan to work on them or to work through them. This will definitely enable us to turn our limitations and challenges into opportunities.

My friend, by knowing your stuff and putting some positive reinforcement behind it—there is no limit on what you can achieve.

People win because they believe that they are winners. People lose because they subconsciously believed they would. Is it a game? Absolutely! There are 2 things that will happen in life:

1. We will win at living our lives the way we desire.
2. We will lose at living our lives the way we desire.

We really create our own reality whether we acknowledge it or not. So, what about the things that happen in our lives that's out of our control? Great question. Things happen to good people and things happen to bad people—the point is, THINGS HAPPEN! Simply, deal with it or don't deal with it, we must adjust our thoughts and determine how we can turn whatever happened into a win-win situation. My friend, no matter how bad it may seem, there is always some good that could be found if we search for it. And, when we stop learning, whatever we are doing starts to decrease. Our best bet, is not to become defensive when others are sharing information with us or when we need to pick up a book to brush up or polish up our skills. The moment we stop learning, we start to become limited.

However, in order to stay on top of our game in marketing, we must find a way to utilize the news media and search engine outlets. Listed below are some of the most popular search engines that you can use to gather valuable information or to market your business:

## Search Engines and Resources

| Alta Vista | Hotbot | Search Engine Watch |
|---|---|---|
| All the Web | Google | Sheppard's Science Resources |
| Dogpile | Lycos | Study Web |
| Excite | Northern Light | Webcrawler |
| Fast Search | Search.com | Yahoo \| Yahooligans |

And, when doing so, here are a few powerful sales words to use:

| | | |
|---|---|---|
| Free | Amazing | Save |
| Suddenly | Wanted | Offer |
| Miracle | Sensational | Introducing |
| Now | Challenge | Quick |
| New | Remarkable | Improvement |
| Magic | Compare | Easy |
| Announcing | Revolutionary | Stop |

| Bargain | Startling | Hurry |
| Guaranteed | Limited Time | How |

These words will help you to market, sale, up-sale and cross-sale your products or services. However, the most successful marketers are the ones who do not juggle 10 things at one time. Until you become an expert, you must focus on one project at a time. This will help keep your budget to a minimum to ensure that you are able to maximize your results. In order to become truly successful at what you are doing, you need to stay focused—this is not the time to lose your momentum. And, regardless of what you do and don't do, finish what you start and start what you can finish while being consistent in all that you do. Now, that you have this information, you must write a different ad each day to place in the online classified sections of the following links:

1. www.craigslist.org
2. www.salespider.com
3. www.webclassifieds.us
4. www.ezclassifieds.com

# Chapter 13

## Leave Your Ego at Home

This is not the time for super-inflated egos. A busted ego has caused more downfalls to greatness than we could ever imagine. Our best bet is to leave our egos at home and bring courage along with us to ensure that fear has no room to attack us when we least expect it. By using this principle, we are better able to help others get what they want without us getting what we want first. Whether we get what we want on the front or back end will not matter if we take our ego out of the equation.

Our thoughts, motives and interests are contributing factors regarding whether or not we are able to maximize our creativity. We are all weak in some area of our life, if you are not—then live a little longer. My friend, in order to overcome our weaknesses, you must maximize your strengths. And, by enhancing a strength, you are then able to diligently work on a weakness without settling for defeat in that particular area of your life. Most often, when our creativity is blocked by a weakness, we tend not to do anything. And, that should give us more of a reason to unblock our creative energy.

My friend, we know exactly when our mind is divided and we know exactly when we want to cry wolf. Crying wolf (playing the victim) may be a great game to play, but when the need for real help presents itself in our life, then what are we going to do? Distractions can and will keep us off-balanced if we do not develop some form of consistency. As a matter of fact, we cannot blame anyone for our impeded progress; because our thoughts, motives and interests contribute to what we attract into and out of our lives. Now, with that being said, work on your weaknesses while maximizing your strengths. This will help you to enhance the true creative force that's inside of you.

If you find yourself at a loss, you must ask questions. You should never be afraid to ask questions when you have access to people who have the answers. My friend, put your pride behind you and ask questions. Put your pride behind you and ask for help. Put your pride behind you and ask why you are not succeeding. Ask. Ask. Ask and ask some more if you are not getting the results that you desire. People will help you when you are determined and willing to help yourself. If you cannot find a person, get on the internet and do some research—the internet has a smorgasbord of great information that will help you. Use the search engines that I provided in the previous chapter to do research; this will help build consistency in your pursuit of getting great information.

Consistency is the inapt ability to follow-through when we are tempted to brush the 'need to do' under the rug. How often are we tempted to sweep things under the rug in order to not deal with them? It is all too often, of course. The best part of our follow-through is being able to consistently follow-up on ourselves. God will meet us at the point of our need—all we need to do is become consistent with being able to follow-up on the people, places and things in our life. And, brushing things under the rug is not the most beneficial way to get rid of anything, it will only cause things to pile up, causing us to attract parasitic relationships that suck the life out of us.

How do you determine who or what's parasitic? They are usually the people, places and things that make you feel bad about your past, or make you feel bad about being who you are. However, it's not limited to feelings; it could also be the people, places and things that hinder your developmental process. And, for that reason, we must follow-up with ourselves, our spouse, our children, our extended family, our friends, our clients, and most of all, we must follow-up with God.

Teaming up with the right people will help us mastermind what it's going to take to get us where we need to be. Who's on your team? Or, better yet, "Who's not on your team?" As you very well know, champions are not born, they are created by a teamified network of people who support what they are doing and what they believe in. Actually, teaming up with the right people helps us to minimize the irritations associated with having the wrong people, places and things in our lives. Regardless, of what we may have to deal with, it is just as important to focus on our network of people as it is to focus on what we need to do daily, weekly, monthly and yearly. When we become indecisive about what we need to do or what we should be doing, we will find ourselves becoming indecisive about the people that we should surround ourselves with. I am not saying that we should think that we are better than anyone—I am saying that we need to become selective about who we allow in our space. If we team up with those who are doing unwise things, we will find ourselves unknowingly doing likewise. And, just because we have an association with someone does not necessarily mean that he or she is on our team, nor does it mean that he or she needs to be on our team for us to benefit from them.

When building a mastermind team, unity is key. Unified minds are better than having someone on your team whose goal is to divide your mind or to divide the unity of the team. Now, in order for you to master what you already have, it's imperative that you team up with people who are doing the same or who have done what you are trying to do. This is not a matter of leaving people out, it's just a matter of selecting the proper ingredients when cooking up your dream and making it a reality! Now, in order to do so, you need the people who are positive and supportive of who you are and not negative or demeaning on your team. Today is your day to get rid of the excess parasitic dirt that's hanging out in your life to threaten your developmental process. Find a mentor or coach and if you can afford a mentor, get one. However, if you cannot afford one, you always have the option of group mentoring at your local Chamber of Commerce.

# Chapter 14
## Leading In The Know

The best way to lead your field is to gain a true understanding of what you desire in and out of life. The greatest leaders are the best followers and the greatest follower has the potential to become the greatest leader. Whether we are leading or following our field, we must know our wants and desires as well as our do not wants and do not desires in life. This will help us to better understand the timing of when to lead and when to follow or vice-versa.

When we know what we do or don't want or desire, we can better relay those same desires to others. However, when we are clueless about these things, we will tend to set up false expectations that are bound to cause us some form of disappointment. It is your responsibility to take a negative and turn it into something positive. And, it is also your responsibility to do what others are not willing to do. The more you lead or follow with integrity, the better you are able to embrace opportunity when it's presented to you.

After people buy you, they want to know what you have to offer and how it's going to benefit them. We must know our product from the inside out! This will help us present the benefits without sounding scripted or fake, even though people buy things day in and day out, they do not like to be sold. They like to be coached. In order to coach effectively, we must know the what, when, where, how and why's of what we are offering them. Furthermore, people buy more of what they want than what they need. So, we must find a way to cater to the want and coach the need to ensure all of our bases are covered, while providing an advantage or a feeling worth remembering. Don't forget to empathize and identify with the wants and needs. When you know your stuff, you are better able to focus on the marketing aspect of your business as it creates more discipline in your life.

The funny thing about discipline is that it creates order in our lives causing us to follow a specific pattern to achieve our desired result. As a matter of fact, discipline leads to perseverance and perseverance leads to us taking baby steps toward our goal, eventually leading up to maneuvering with ease and achieving the desires of our heart. As we all know, success will always come with a price tag. Most often, the price will consist of remaining calm when things get out of control. Our ability to keep our composure in the midst of a storm creates a form of strength that others will not be able to understand, especially when we are able to succeed under pressure. Just don't forget to learn from the storm because every storm has a lesson, with every lesson comes more discipline and with more discipline comes SUCCESS!

There are many misconceptions in life and discipline is not one of them. When we allow ourselves to meander through life doing whatever we want without any accountability, we are setting ourselves up for the ultimate disappointment. Discipline is required to achieve anything worth having and without it, we will not get much accomplished. When we find ourselves surrounded by incomplete projects, incomplete relationships or incomplete anything, our guard should automatically go up. This is a sign of having too many distractions and too many distractions impede our discipline. Furthermore, the lack of discipline leaves room for bad habits to take over and control our lives; and, the one thing we must never do is, lose our ability to govern ourselves mentally, physically, emotionally or spiritually. This will ensure that we are able to build, break-down, restore, preserve or burn a bridge if necessary, depending on our situation or circumstance at hand.

It's okay to lift your head above the crowd to see more than what everyone else is looking at! And, even when things do not go your way, you must look at things from a different perspective. This will definitely empower you to start what you can finish and finish what you start.

# *Chapter 15*

## *Limitless Potential*

Listening is one of the greatest gifts known to man, without it we become limited. Furthermore, we can definitely hear more when we listen opposed to talking. As I said before, people will tell you how they want to be sold and they will also tell you why you need to share information with them. They know what they are looking for better than anyone else, and all we have to do is "Break the ice." And, this can be done by asking fact finding-questions and repeating back to them what you have heard. This will tell them that you were paying attention to them. And, when you have their atttention, share what you can and will do for them, while assuming the sale by asking for it.

Utilizing the positive impact of listening and learning will prevent our growth from becoming stunted in asking for the sale or asking for the money. When we stop learning new things, we may have a hard time finding new and improved ways of selling or sharing our product or service. We are designed to learn, grow and become more than what we are today. As you know, we all want to become successful at something whether we admit to it or not. Now, in order for us to become successful at something, we must listen and learn from other successful people.

Learning more is not always a common practice for everyone. The individuals who tend to refuse to learn more of what they don't know will eventually become closed-minded to change. In so many words, they will start resisting change when change is inevitable. When you positively think through, strategize, prioritize and learn, there is no limit on what you can achieve. As a matter of fact, that's a powerful combination that will have a lasting effect on you as well as those around you giving more structure and stability in your life.

Structure helps us to streamline our ability to persist at things that pose some form of resistance. Structure is well needed in our lives, especially when it comes down to knowing what we don't want and what we do. Having structure in our lives will help us to think about things before we take action. Of course, we will not be able to please everyone 100% of the time, we will not be right 100% of the time nor will we be wrong 100% of the time; but, we can exercise our integrity 100% of the time. However, when we have structure backed by our integrity we are better equipped to overcome the resistant places in our lives.

When it comes down to marketing yourself, your product or service, why stress ourselves out over people, places and things, when structure is designed to put them into the proper perspective. Just remember, people, places and things come into your life for a reason and they will also exit your life for a reason as well. And, with that being said, I want you to maximize every moment, taking what you need from life and discarding the rest. Lastly, when it comes down to the structure that you have in your life, what's going on outside of you is just as important as what's going on inside of you. So, take a minute to evaluate what you allow into your space and what you are going to get rid of to ensure that your marketing becomes effective.

# Chapter 16

## Learning Through Objection

When we base our success totally upon what we know and not upon overcoming an objection, we will eventually become stagnate. Stagnated success causes more undue pressure than not becoming successful at all. And, when this happens, it can and will seep over into other areas of our lives creating more havoc than we care to bear.

In whatever you do, always add learning into the equations to prevent yourself from becoming stuck in a rut or stuck in your own way of doing things. As you very well know, the more you learn, the more you grow and the more you take action while growing, the more you can accomplish and the more money you will make. So, regardless of how minute your accomplishments may seem, learn, learn and learn some more. Hint, hint, sharing gives what you have learned power and it also gives it ACTION! Putting what you have learned in motion activates the law of reciprocity; therefore, keeping the floodgates of knowledge open to you to ensure that you are able to successfully overcome objections.

When we get to know our own emotions, goals and ambitions, we are then able to turn rejection or failure into opportunity. Against all odds, small accomplishments do add up when we become disciplined in our actions and emotions. In some minute way, life gives us an opportunity to cherish or perish in what we have or do, based on how we feel and react to the people, places and things around us. Of course, the complexities of life will come; but, it is how we deal with the emotional aspect of rejection and failure that will determine whether our battles are won or lost.

Rejection and failure are the two main obstacles that are designed to block us in our time of need. And, regardless of what we say or do, someone will have something to say and everyone will have their own opinion, such as life! However, we cannot allow the judgments and the opinions of others to affect us emotionally; but we can allow the judgments and the opinions of others to motivate, encourage and strengthen us to embrace opportunity. We can do anything or accomplish any goal by determining the level of our emotional wants or needs, and how we resolve conflict when we are stressed out.

My friend, whenever tackling issues, make sure that you calm down, pray, meditate on the issue and then attempt to resolve it. What if you don't have enough time? Great question, you are just going to have to go through the process really quick. Once you get use to the process, it becomes a lot easier. And, when you want something bad enough, you must take your eyes off the obstacle and place it on your goal, dream or ambition and use your faith to take care of the supernatural side of it. It's that simple! Do what you do best, let nothing paralyze you and leave the rest up to God.

When we are able to overcome the objections in life, we will no longer be bound by the desire to doubt. Objections come and objections go, what would we do without them? There are many different types of positive and negative objections that are designed to create doubt. Frankly, where there is doubt, there is also an unanswered question to keep us confused and frustrated over people, places and things that may or may not change.

An unanswered question about an objection can be worked out with a plan of action. As I always say, "When in doubt, write it out." There will always be a solution to an objection; it just may or may not be the solution that we want. But, for the most part, how we handle objections will determine the emotional role that rejection will play in our lives. However, the true uncut solution will most often be what we need at the time, regardless of whether we feel rejected or not. Trust me, the sting of rejection will soon fade if we accept or acknowledge the objection without doubting as we move forward with confidence.

Most often, when we get a "NO" that means that they don't have enough information. In so many words, they are not convinced by the information that you have provided them with. And, whether you are the prime source of the objection or not, never allow an objection to cause you to give up. All it means is that you need to go back to the drawing table on how to overcome an objection. If you are able to master the reason that they did not purchase what you had to offer, you will become better able to overcome the next objection with ease. Besides, your strength is gained when you humbly stand your ground without doubting what and whom you believe in.

The survival of the fittest comes into play when we make the appropriate adjustments to accommodate rejection or an objection in order to negotiate. The power of negotiation works when we have our integrity intact. As a matter of fact, our negotiation skills are greatly enhanced when we master our conflict resolution to incorporate a positive twist. We are able to pretty much create anything that we desire as long as we are able to extract the positive and use the negative as a learning tool to enhance our strategic thinking process. When we know and understand who we are, what we want, and why we want it—we are better able to make the necessary adjustments to accommodate the situations or circumstances at hand without beguiling anyone or anything to get what we want. Furthermore, negotiating with an ulterior motive is a quick way to put a ripple effect in our integrity; regardless of whether we value it or not. When we are upfront and honest about our intents, we are able to earn more respect from those who are easily scorned. Everything is not negotiable especially when your integrity is hanging in the balance.

Our unparallel sacrifices are usually made in the areas in which we lack discipline or the areas that we knowingly or unknowingly squander. Wasting time is definitely listed on all of our resumes at some point in our lives. However, when we continue to squander precious time, we will find that we are at a loss for something that will eventually cause us to become codependent. Regardless of whether we are codependent or interdependent, there is nothing better than having our own. Now, in order to have our own, we must become disciplined in our actions and reactions—whether that action is in prayer, fasting, working longer, harder or smarter, etc., discipline is a must! And, with that being said, anything or anybody that's worth having, should be worth the sacrifice; if they are not—then we are definitely wasting our time.

When we choose to move forward in greatness, we will; and, until we are ready, we will remain where we are or where we have been. Furthermore, if we really want to know and understand the choices that we have made, simply evaluate our actions, reactions, and activities. Trust me, they will reveal our choice(s) without anyone saying one word. Limitations are created in the mind when there is codependency residing in our heart. And, for that reason alone, this is not the time to become closed-minded! Everyone may not be going where you are going, they may not look the way you want them to look and they may not have what you expect them to have. Trust me, there is always something to learn from a person who maintains a focused and positive outlook on life. You should always remind yourself that you possess unlimited potential, regardless of the opinion or the judgment of others. When you do this, it enables you to become interdependent, allowing everyone to play his or her role in your life.

# Chapter 17

## Marketing Channels Made Easy

There is a time and a season for everything. And, regardless of whether it's the right time or the wrong time, time is always on our side whether we think so or not. Time is not what fails us, it's our inability to recognize that time has been designed to govern our lives and to keep everything on track. Against all odds with a little time, small accomplishments do add up. Furthermore, anything that we work on long enough with discipline, action, and commitment, in time—we can and will master or become an expert at whatever it is.

At any rate, positively do what you do best and leave the rest up to God. So the next time you instantly become frustrated, angry, irritated, lost or confused, take a minute to ask yourself why and evaluate the situation or circumstance accordingly. Whether the reason is known or unknown, you are the best positive YOU that you have. And, it takes TIME to release the true winner that's inside of you.

We are all a work in progress and it's so easy to pass the buck of blame; actually, it feels good not to have to assume responsibility for our mistakes. Finding the point of our error is a great way to find a resolution; therefore, making problem-solving a little easier. Of course, we often do not like to admit that we need to work on certain things in our life; however, the denial of the things that we need to work on can and will drive a wedge through some area of our life. My friend, the first step to solving our issues whether we think we have them or not, is to assume the responsibility for our role in any given situation or circumstance. Although, there is good and bad in everyone--we must find a way to supersede the bad to ensure that we do not fall into the trap of blaming others for things that we choose not to take responsibility for. In order to assume responsibility for maximizing your marketing dollars, there are a few things that you must know:

1. You must know who's in the market.
2. You must know how they are promoting their business.
3. You must know how they target clients.
4. You must know their price range.
5. You must know and understand their success and failures.
6. You must know what the market is calling for.
7. You must know the strengths and weaknesses of the market.
8. You must know your place in the market.
9. You must know the potential threats.
10. You must know why you are in the market.
11. You must know the need of what you are offering.
12. You must know what is costing you to be in the market.
13. You must know your specialty.
14. You must know how you are going to target the market.
15. You must know what's going to make you different.
16. You must know your potential clients.

17. You must know if a company will sponsor your product or service.
18. You must know your point of uniqueness.
19. You must know what potential clients are expecting from you.
20. You must know what you are and are not willing to do.
21. You must know how to test the validity of the product and service that you are selling.
22. You must be willing to negotiate in the heat of the moment.
23. You must know your limits.
24. You must know how to agree and proceed.
25. You must know how to sell or promote your service with the feel, felt, found theory.
26. You must be willing to walk away from people, places and things that violate your integrity or the integrity of your product or service.
27. You must know how to remain calm when promoting or selling your product or service.

Here are some great ways to promote your business with little or no upfront cost:

| | |
|---|---|
| Press Releases | Yellow pages |
| Prospecting | Classified ads |
| Social Events | Magazines |
| Youtube | Radio |
| Facebook | Television |
| Twitter | Billboard |
| My Space | Direct mail |
| Research Surveys | Pens |
| News Letters | Samples CD's |
| Quotes | Seminars |
| Blogs | Sponsoring events |
| Workshops | Trade shows |
| Questionnaires | T-shirts |
| Writing articles | Word of mouth advertising |
| Wanted ads | Give free gifts |
| Letters | Email campaigns |
| Email | Press Releases |
| Faxes | Circulars |
| Brochures | Post fliers |

# Chapter 18
## How to Protect Your Promise or Gift

The driving force of our passion resides in our ability to dedicate ourselves to that in which is destined to challenge us. The dynamics of achieving success in anything or with anyone, requires us to persevere through our challenges to achieve a common goal. Now, whatever that common goal is—is up to you.

Everything that we do, say, or react to, contributes to the way in which we deal with ourselves, as well as the way in which we deal with or help others. As we all know, challenges will come and challenges will go; and we must determine what we hold on to when the challenges leave—some hold on to resentment, some hold on to anger, some hold on to fear and some hold on to the ability to let go.  Regardless of what we hold on to, we are held accountable for what we do with and how we react to our experiences.  My friend, you are here to make a difference!  It is through you that a certain amount of people can be reached and it's your responsibility to make a positive impact on them, regardless of your set of challenges.

When we find the common denominator of our problem in our ability to market effectively, we are then better able to find a solution without losing our integrity.  Whether we are on the high-end or the low-end of life, we will all have something that we need to work on.  Whether it's the highest common denominator or the lowest, our best bet is to find out the what's, when's, where's, how's and why's of our marketing plan to ensure that we do not fall by the wayside, wasting our money, time and effort.  Of course, we may not have all the answers to everything in life, but we definitely have an idea regarding most things; especially, when most of our solutions are hidden deep within us.

We must take the time to evaluate what went wrong, in order to make things go right. Of course, no one likes to be wrong, and self correction can become difficult at times. However, when we do not know or understand the problem behind our decisions or mistakes then we subject ourselves to the aftereffect of compromise when our back is up against the wall. The key to building strength is to keep trying, without giving up on Y.O.U. Finding the common denominator in your successes and failures in life really prepares you to go to the next level without regretting the process of doing so. And, regardless of where you are in life, follow-up is key. When you master your ability to follow-up on yourself in all that you do, say and become—you will find that you are able to follow-through without losing your grip on your integrity by doing a few things such as:

1. Value your privacy. People will deplete you of all your energy if you allow them to.
2. Guard your thoughts. Your thoughts create your reality.
3. Focus on the wants and not the DON'T WANTS.
4. Be cautious about where you get your information.
5. Exercise caution regarding who you allow into your life.

6. Know that your potential can cause the actual.
7. Consider yourself blessed at all times.
8. Never become afraid to say goodbye to the past and hello to your future.
9. Understand that you have been chosen for your own unique assignment.
10. Plan your life to create a wall of success.

# Chapter 19
## Your Choice

Successful abundance is at its best when we make the necessary adjustments in our action plan to reach our maximum potential. Continuing to do the same thing, expecting a different result is not wise. We need to change things up from time-to-time in order to reach our maximum potential. And, by doing so, there is no need to waste time and energy on something that's not working or something that's bringing about defeat. Now, in order to successfully create abundance in our lives, we must spend more time and energy changing our approach to why people, places and things are not working in our lives. Once we analyze our approach, we are better able to determine the necessary changes.

Choices are a part of life, when we do not make wise choices—it becomes quite evident in our lives. Of course, we are not able to fix everything, but we can determine why something is not working and make a decision, if need be. My friend, this is where our flexibility is established. There are going to be times when we need to change our plan of action; however, the recognition of the change is of great importance. We must recognize and commit to change before the change can actually take place. Changing something that we feel as if change is not necessary, creates a double-negative; therefore, making change or the transition very difficult.

When you want something bad enough, you will make the changes necessary to get what you want or get rid of what you don't want. Choices are not hard at all—they just require a commitment to know what you need and don't need in your life. My friend, even if you are having a difficult time with change, prayer will change things. And, regardless of where you are right now in your prayer life, simply ask for help. It is one of the most effective tools used in the process of change; yet, it is the most overlooked and the most misunderstood! Today, embrace the essence of your change to ensure that your life becomes a representation of wise choices.

Our personal limitations will make us feel as if a choice is a chore, when it's just a positive or negative commitment to self. How often do we make choices difficult? More than we care to imagine, right? My friend, our decision making process is essential in the way in which we would like to reap the fruits of our labor.

Most often, we do not make a choice because we have not really made up our mind about something or someone. Of course, choices do become difficult, especially when we are confused about what we want or do not want in our lives; and, even more confusing when there is a bad habit involved. However, bad habits can become good if we know and understand the underlying reason that the habit became bad in the first place. My friend, listen to me and listen to me well, whatever you want out of life is not going to happen by chance, it is going to happen by CHOICE. As of today, start making wise choices and watch how the windows of opportunity swing wide open.

List 5 things that you would like to change about your life?

1.

2.

3.

4.

5.

List 5 ways to implement these changes in your life?

1.

2.

3.

4.

5.

What have you been procrastinating about lately? List 5 items.

1.

2.

3.

4.

5.


What are your strengths?  List 5 items.

1.

2.

3.

4.

5.

What are your weaknesses?  List 5 items.

1.

2.

3.

4.

5.


What can you do to enable your weaknesses to become strengths?

1.

2.

3.

4.

5.

What does value mean to you?

What type of value do you place on yourself?

What is your worth?

# Chapter 20
## Communication Savvy

When perfecting our marketing skills listed below are a few things we must take into consideration:

1. **Image.** Although, we don't like to admit that image plays a vital role; however, it will often determine a sale or no sale.
2. **Business Savvy.** When marketing, you must appear organized while knowing the product or service that you are presenting.
3. **Communication.** We must learn how to speak the language of our client or customer. If we speak beyond what they can comprehend, we may lose them as a

customer. If we speak below his or her level of comprehension, we put ourselves at risk of losing a client as well. And, using slang is a NO-NO.

4. **Trustworthiness.** Our clients need to trust us. Our trustworthiness is displayed in the type of service that we provide. If we are efficient, respectful, compassionate and competent, our clients will trust our product or service.

5. **Maturity.** I encourage having fun with clients; however, we must not act immature around our clients or have too many drinks. This is a quick way to lose our credibility.

6. **Mannerism.** It's imperative that we use proper business etiquette around our clients. We must be courteous to our clients on the phone or in person, building value in the relationship.

Unprofessional behavior is a quick way to distort the communication between you and a client. Once the communication is lost with self, rest assured that it will trickle down to other areas of your life. Therefore, making it imperative that you work on self and then on to perfecting your communications skills with others. Listed below are a few questions to perfect the way in which you are communicating:

**How effective is your communication?**

**How do you affect others when you speak?**

**What do you talk about?**

**Are your conversations positive or negative?**

**Do you always have to be right in every conversation?**

Do you always have the last word in every conversation?

Are you exerting too much energy trying to defend yourself?

Do you think about what you are going to say before you say it?

Do you motivate, encourage or build up others when you speak?

Do you listen when others respond to your questions or comments?

How are you responding to conflict or a stressful situation?

Make a list of the words that you need to eliminate from your vocabulary:

What do you want your foundation to consist of?

Are you willing to pray on a daily basis or pray before you start communicating with others?

# Chapter 21

## Repertoire of Greatness

Hard work will drive anyone to create their own repertoire of greatness while being mentored to the top. Who doesn't want to be great? We all do, even if we don't want to admit it. Our repertoire of greatness is within our reach as long as we are willing to work for it. As we all know, the fruits of our labor require hard work, dedication, accountability and a positive attitude. Good potential that's not acted upon is what? An unpurposeful potential! When we find a purpose for our potential, then we are better able to govern the change of it or the redirection of the energy pertaining to it. Frankly, we must focus on being consistent and committed to what we are doing. And, the best way to do that is to find a mentor or coach. In my opinion, they are able to fine-tune what you already have and they will help to keep you from lying to yourself.

Most successful people have a coach to help them to become and remain accountable for what they are doing and what they are not doing. When we are not accountable for something, we tend to become a little lazy or we will tend to put things off. My friend, it's extremely hard to become lazy when our mentor or coach is holding us accountable for our developmental process. As you very well know, we are not born with the ability to achieve peak performance, it is developed. We have a few great abilities that often go over looked and they are:

1. Our ability to become teachable.
2. Our ability to learn.
3. Our ability to share.

Once we are learnable, teachable and sharable, we have a great combination that could achieve anything with the proper mentoring. Having one without the other will cause us to become limited.

Who wants to work hard and have our efforts blocked for the same amount of energy? No one, of course. So, it is better to get rid of anything that has the potential of hindering our progress to ensure that we are able to maximize our abilities without squandering them. I do understand that the average person may not be able to afford a coach; however, we are able to pick up a book to start, while working our way up to seminars and workshops or a coach.

Now, with that being said, surround yourself with people that can help you, develop you and nurture you into greatness without having an ulterior motive. Make no mistake about it, it is quite okay to surround yourself with intelligent, committed, and trustworthy people that will help feed your vision, while helping you meet and exceed the expectations that you may have set for yourself. And, when you do, regardless of what obstacle you may face, you will rise to the top—life is designed that way!

# Chapter 22

## Praying your way to the Top

The milestone of our excellency is determined by our attitude of effectiveness, as well as our ability to pray over and pray through events, situations, and circumstances. Now, let me ask you, "How effective are you?" The efficiency of our effectiveness has a great impact on where we are going and how we are going to get there. Our behavior is a tell-tell sign of what we are thinking. If we do things in the spirit of excellence—our thoughts are of excellency. If we just throw things together—our thoughts will reflect that as well. The ultimate life performance factors are based upon our ability to decide, do, become, participate, negotiate and resolve. These 6 factors will help us to prepare and overcome obstacles that are designed to get us off balance. My friend, using positive affirmations is the quickest way to change our negative thought patterns. As a matter of fact, when we become accountable for our effectiveness, we are better able to determine our will-power of excellence. When you acknowledge and work on your short-comings, you are better able to maximize your strengths without panicking over things that may or may not happen. Besides, you cannot go wrong doing everything in the spirit of excellence with a genuine cover of an integrity-filled prayer.

Successful People pray for guidance. Prayer has a dynamic way of strengthening our backbone to ensure that we are able to stand up straight without falling for the okey-doke. Patience, faith and prayer are key players in finding the right solution to any situation or problem. Patience is the ability to endure your pains, stresses or hardships calmly and without complaint. Impatience is the opposite; it is the inability to cope with pains, stresses and hardships. As a matter of fact, impatience is not of God—I know that it is human nature to want an immediate answer in a time of heartache and trial;

but, rest assured that God will not rush us into making any unwise decisions. It is the trick of the enemy that tries to push us into getting ahead of God by making a decision quickly. On the other hand, God knows what He's doing, and He uses the tool called time to accomplish His great works to prevent us from making a mess of our lives. And, for that reason, we must create a system to keep our faith in tack.

Anything worth having is worth putting a system in place. In order to better understand the people, places and things that are working for us or working against us, it's imperative that we know and understand the plan of direction that we have set for our own life. Therefore, giving us an opportunity to use our faith to adapt and survive through a situation, circumstance or event that has been designed to knock us off our feet. With all that being said, a faithful systematic plan will always take you further than a clueless or skeptical one.

Persistence is the key to treading upon uncharted territory. Sometimes God will make a way out of no way, but there are times when God requires us to exhaust all of our resources first or to make do with what we have. Today, find your niche, get you a system and work it while making your prayer request known. Write out 10 requests that you would like God to do for you.

## Prayer Requests

1. _____

2. _____

3. _____

4. _____

5. _____

6. _____

7. _____

8. _____

9. _____

10. _____

# PRAYER CONTRACT:

I, _____, will devote time out for prayer every morning at _____ and every evening at _____. This will be my time with God in Prayer for the next 30 days.

_____
**Signature**

# Chapter 23

## Keeping Record

A journal's greatest benefit is being able to express yourself without anyone passing judgment against you. Journalizing your thoughts, desires, goals, and prayers, can really show the nature of God. Nevertheless, don't be afraid to write down your feelings of pain, sorrow, frustration, disappointment, or anger. The key to journaling is to be able to express your feelings without any guilt or shame about any situation or circumstance. Your journal will become your daily record of what happens to you throughout your day, whether it's good or bad.

If you don't write a journal, you might forget about the great works of God. Write a journal with an intent on sharing it with yourself, so that you can recall the mountains that God has moved for you. This journal is your personal property; it will become one of your greatest assets as you open the doors of your intimate expressions to God. Without a doubt, get ready for the confirmation of His great love for you.

At the beginning of each week, you will need to list your weekly goals, accomplishments and set-backs. This way, you are able to evaluate your progress or the areas that you need to work on. Get a pocketsize journal to keep with you at all times and transfer it to your regular journal daily.

# Chapter 24

## Ignition

Dreams do come true when we understand the underlying passion that resides from within while getting rid of our false expectations. False expectations create an imbalance in the heart and mind when we try to override the cause and effect in our lives. When our beliefs and expectations are not matching up, that is an indication that there very well may be some false expectations that are not lining up with what we believe in our heart and what we see in our mind. My friend, everything happens for a reason; therefore, it's imperative that we make sure that what we are thinking about is lining up with what we are doing.

Our personal limitations hold us back more than anything else known to man. When our mindset becomes stagnant, rest assured that failure is right around the corner waiting for us. An ignited passion requires an enhanced or new mind-set to ensure that we are able to concentrate on what we are creating. And, as long as our vision, desires, beliefs, goals and emotions do not violate the will of someone else, we are free to believe what we want. Hopefully, it would have a positive impact; however, it could have a negative effect as well. So, be very cautious, when stepping on someone's toes or when burning bridges when embarking upon our dream.

We must become sincerely focused on what we are doing and not waste time and energy on making excuses for not doing. Taking action is the fuel that can and will feed that burning desire from within. When we decide to lead our own life, we are better able to determine how far we are going to take the passion that's inside of us. People cannot stop that in which we believe in; although, they may hinder us if we become indecisive. My friend, no one can stop the unlimited potential that resides in those who are focused and committed to that burning desire from within. As a matter of fact, when a purpose is known and we are able to ignite the passion behind it—successful wealth will come knocking at our door.

Victorious living is within your reach. All you have to do is stay focused with a positive attitude, while having an idea of what, when, how, where and why you are moving. Soon enough, victory will come knocking at your door. The last thing you ever want to do is wallow in self-pity when it's so easy to gird up your loins and walk or flow in victorious living. From me to you, it's not the way in which you tell your story that creates victory; it is the way in which you LIVE your story that creates victory. This is "Millionaire Hustle" at its best—So, get up, go out and make millions. Be Blessed and Be a Blessing to Someone Else.

Koocie Montgomery

# Marketing Resource Index

For domain names, websites or webmail go to:
www.godaddy.com

To build and host your own website go to:
www.Homestead.com
www.godaddy.com

Set up Newsletter or Email Blasts:
www.ConstantContact.com

To sell digital eBooks go to:
www.payloadz.com

Accept Credit Cards through:
www.propay.com or www.paypal.com

Merchant Account through:
www.FirstData.com
www.paypal.com

Arrange Conference calls for free:
www.Freeconferencecall.com

Free Promotional Banners:
www.AdDesigner.com
Affiliate Links:

www.ClickBank.com

Write Articles:
www.ezinearticles.com
www.examiner.com

Purchase Royalty-free photos:
www.istock.com

Sell products:
www.ebay.com
www.Craigslist.org
www.Amazon.com